Beyond the Veil

REFLECTIONS ON
TRUTH & CONSCIOUSNESS

A POETRY COLLECTION

DREW MACKBY SAND

Beyond the Veil © Drew Mackby Sand, 2025

All rights reserved. No part of this book may be reproduced, stored in a retrieval system, or transmitted in any form or by any means, electronic or mechanical, without the prior written permission of the publisher, except in the case of brief quotations embodied in critical reviews and articles.

This book is intended for informational and artistic purposes only. The content reflects the author's personal insights and creative expressions and should not be considered a substitute for professional advice or guidance.

First Edition: 2025
A catalogue record of this book is available with *Library and Archives Canada.*

Independently Published
Author: *Drew Mackby Sand*
Title: *Beyond the Veil*
ISBN: 978-1-0690582-3-2

I just wanted to express how I feel—
to give shape to the unseen,
to speak what lingers beyond words,
to reach those who feel the pull beyond the veil.

This is for you.

Preface

There comes a time in every soul's journey when the illusion begins to crack—when the stories we've been told no longer hold weight, and the quiet knowing within us grows louder than the world's distractions. This collection is born from that space—the threshold between what was and what is becoming.

These are not simply words on a page, nor are they meant to be read passively. They are invitations, echoes, transmissions from a deeper place. They are reflections of the questions we ask in silence, the truths that linger in the spaces between thoughts.

If you are here, it is no accident. Whether you are unraveling, awakening, remembering, or simply seeking something beyond the surface, these words have found you for a reason. You may feel challenged. You may feel seen. You may feel the mind resisting what the soul already knows. Good. That means you are shifting, expanding, stepping into something more.

This is not a book to be consumed in one sitting. It is an unfolding. A mirror. A call back to yourself.

Take what resonates. Let the rest drift like leaves in the wind.

Welcome. I see you. I honor you.

—*Drew Mackby Sand*

A Seed's Promise

You are but a seed,
rooted in the soil of your being,
waiting for the rain of love
to awaken you.
Trust in the process,
for all that you seek
is already within.

The Power in Now

In this moment,
the past is but a shadow,
the future, a mere whisper.
Only now is real—
the breath you take,
the heart you feel,
the steps you take in this very second.

Let go of all that binds you
to what was,
and embrace what is.

The Weight of Silence

The quiet speaks louder
than words ever could.
It hums a melody of truth
in the spaces between,
where sound fails to reach.

We fill the void with noise,
but it is the silence
that carries the deepest weight.

The Alchemy of Being

You are the alchemist,
the magician of your soul.
Transform pain into wisdom,
grief into strength,
and joy into light.

The world is your canvas,
and you are the brush.

Let Them Be

Let them go.
Let them choose.
Let them walk their own path,
even if it twists away from yours.

Not everything needs your hands to fix,
nor your voice to correct.
Not every battle is yours to fight,
not every mind yours to change.

Let them believe what they believe.
Let them do as they will.
Let them make mistakes,
grow at their own pace.

The more you release,
the lighter you become.
The less you grip,
the freer you feel.

Peace is found in surrender,
not in control.
Freedom is found in allowing,
not in forcing.

So let them go.
Let them be.
And in doing so,
set yourself free.

When Shadows Speak

Shadows stretch long
as the day turns to dusk,
but in their silence,
they speak the loudest truths.

Fear not the dark,
for it holds the wisdom
that the light cannot show.

BEYOND THE VEIL

The Path Unknown

The path ahead is fogged,
but you are not lost.
Trust the rhythm of your steps,
and let the unknown be your guide.

Each moment leads you home,
even if you cannot yet see
the way.

The Unspoken Truth

There is a truth
you will never find in words.
It is felt, not spoken,
seen, not told.

Trust the wisdom of your heart
and let it lead you,
for the truth you seek
has always been with you.

A Quiet Strength

Strength does not always roar.
It is in the quiet moments,
the steady breath,
the courage to stand still
when the world pushes you to move.

The Language of Love

Love speaks in silence,
in gestures small and tender.
It does not need words to be heard,
for its voice is felt
in the heartbeat shared
and the connection between souls.

The Dance of Impermanence

Everything you love
is like a leaf caught in the wind,
whirling, spinning,
and then it falls.

We grip too tightly
to things that will eventually slip
through our fingers.
But in letting go,
we learn the dance of impermanence,
and find peace in the flow of it all.

Your Heart Whispers

Awaken to the sound
of your own heart.
It's been there all along—
the beat, the rhythm,
waiting for you to listen.

The world will scream,
but only in silence
can you hear the truth.

The Essence of Being

You are not your thoughts,
not the roles you play,
not the labels others give you.
You are the essence
that lives beyond all of it,
a spark of the divine
that no words can capture.
Just breathe,
and be.

Trust the Unseen

Do not fear the invisible,
for it is the unseen
that shapes the visible.
Trust the energy around you—
it is the thread
that weaves your story,
even when you cannot see
the pattern.

Echoes of the Soul

Every step you take
echoes in eternity.
Your actions ripple through time,
and though you may not hear it,
the world responds.
Like a stone thrown into water,
the waves of your soul reach far
beyond what you can see.

The Mirror of Nature

Look to the trees,
how they grow,
how they bend in the storm,
how they lose their leaves
and stand tall again.

They reflect the truth of our own nature—
that we too are capable of renewal,
of resilience,
of becoming whole again
with every season.

Unraveling the Self

Peel back the layers
of what you think you are.
There is no end,
only depth.

At the core of it all,
there is no one to be found—
only the vastness of the universe
pouring itself into form.

Rest in the Moment

We are so often caught in the race,
chasing what lies ahead,
but the treasure lies here—
in this breath,
this second,
this stillness.

Rest in the moment,
for it is all you truly need.

The Journey Within

The greatest journey is not across the world,
but into your own soul.
There, you will find the mountains you've climbed,
the rivers you've crossed,
and the depths of your own heart—
a vast landscape of possibility,
waiting to be discovered.

The Quiet Power of Kindness

Kindness does not shout.
It does not demand attention.
It is the quiet hand extended
when no one is looking.
It is the warmth of a smile
given freely,
the soft word
that heals a wound.

In its simplicity,
kindness holds the power
to change the world.

The Weight of Time

Time does not ask for permission.
It moves forward,
quietly, steadily,
like the river carving its path.
We hold onto it,
try to control it,
but in the end,
it slips through our fingers.

Learn to let go,
and feel the weight of time
lighten into a breath,
into a moment.

A Quiet Revolution

It doesn't always have to be loud,
this revolution.
Sometimes, the quietest shifts
create the most profound change.
A soft word,
a single act of kindness,
a thought that sparks transformation.
The world moves in whispers
more than it does in roars.

The Weightless Sky

In the sky, there is no burden—
no heaviness.
The clouds float,
the birds soar,
and the winds carry them
without resistance.

Why, then, do we carry the weight of the world
on our shoulders?
We were meant to fly,
to be light as air.

The Healing Waters

Let the waters of your soul flow,
unclogged by the rocks of fear and doubt.
There is power in the current,
a healing energy that knows no bounds.
When you surrender to it,
you will be carried,
gently,
back to the shore of yourself.

In the Silence

In the silence,
you will hear your truth.
Not in the noise of the world,
but in the quiet,
where the answers reside
like treasures buried beneath the earth.

The Dance of Shadows

The shadows teach us
not to fear the darkness,
but to embrace it.
For without the dark,
there can be no light.
They are partners in a dance,
each one giving shape
to the other.

The Seed of Change

Every thought is a seed,
and every action, a root.
Plant with care,
for you are shaping your world
with each moment.

The garden will grow,
whether you tend it or not.
It is your choice to cultivate it
into something beautiful.

The Space Between

It's not the destination
that matters most,
but the space between.
The in-between moments,
where everything changes,
where growth happens quietly,
where your soul expands
in ways you cannot see.
Embrace the in-between.

Reflections on the Water

Look into the water,
and see not just the reflection,
but the depth beneath.
You are not just surface,
not just what is seen.
There is a whole ocean inside of you,
waiting to be discovered.

The Language of Stars

The stars do not speak,
but they whisper.
Their light speaks to us
in languages we cannot hear
but feel deeply within.
They tell us we are not alone,
that we are a part of something
vast, eternal,
a connection to the cosmos,
always shining,
always guiding.

BEYOND THE VEIL

The Quiet Force

It is not always the loudest voices
that create the most change.
Sometimes, the quietest movements
are the most powerful—
the ones that ripple out,
soft and unnoticed,
until they have reshaped everything.
A single act of love,
a whisper of understanding,
a moment of patience.
These are the forces
that can move mountains,
when given time to grow.

A Breath Between Worlds

There is a moment between every breath
where you are not bound by time,
where the past and future cease to exist,
and you are infinite.
In that space,
you are pure possibility.
You are the present,
untouched by any other.

Breathe into it,
and feel the world unfold
in the pause between.

Stillness in Motion

We often mistake stillness for stagnation,
but stillness is not a lack of movement.
It is the quiet center
from which all motion originates.
The ocean does not stop moving
when it is calm.
The trees do not stop growing
when they stand still.

Stillness is the space
where everything is born from,
where your deepest thoughts
and dreams take root.

The Mountain Within

There is a mountain inside of you,
steep, jagged,
tall enough to touch the sky.
You may not always see it,
but it is there,
silent and steadfast,
waiting to be climbed.
You are not defined by the path you take,
but by the strength you find
within yourself,
each step forging your way
upward,
closer to your own summit.

The Dance of the Seasons

Change is inevitable.
Like the seasons,
it comes,
bringing growth in its wake,
and sometimes,
it brings quiet,
a rest.
We are bound to the rhythm of the Earth,
not as masters,
but as partners.
We too must know when to grow,
and when to rest,
when to push forward,
and when to allow the quiet to settle in.

The dance of seasons is not one of control,
but of trust.

The Light in the Storm

It is easy to see the storm
and forget that the light is still there.
The sun has not gone anywhere,
but is simply hidden behind the clouds.
In the midst of the chaos,
remember that the storm is temporary,
but the light is always present,
always waiting to break through.
You, too, are that light.
Even when life clouds your vision,
you remain steadfast,
a beacon of clarity
waiting for the clouds to part.

The Weight of the Heart

The heart is a heavy thing—
it carries the weight of love,
grief,
joy,
hope.
It bears it all without breaking.
But even the strongest heart needs rest.
Even the most resilient spirit
must pause,
and let go of the burdens it carries.
To truly live,
we must sometimes allow ourselves
to be light again,
to unclench our fists
and release the things
that no longer serve us.

Unspoken Words

There are words that go unsaid
and yet they echo the loudest.
The silence between two souls
can speak volumes,
carrying meaning deeper than any sentence could.
It is in these spaces—
the words you don't say,
the things you feel without speaking—
that you find the truest connection.
Some truths are too vast for language.
They must be felt,
not heard.

The Call to Return

We were born of the Earth,
and to the Earth,
we shall return.
But between birth and death,
we journey.
We forget,
we seek,
we wander,
until one day we hear the call—
the call to return to the source,
to return to the place
where we began.
This journey is not a straight line,
but a spiral that leads us home.

The Unseen Threads

Everything is connected,
though we often fail to see the threads
that bind us.
We touch the lives of others,
leave an imprint on their hearts,
whether we realize it or not.
In the smallest acts—
a smile,
a word,
a gesture of kindness—
we weave the fabric of this world.
And though we may not always see the whole design,
we are always part of it.
Always creating it.

The Gift of Letting Go

To let go is not to forget,
but to release the hold
of what no longer serves you.
It is not weakness,
but strength—
the ability to stand in the present
and say,
"I am free from what binds me."
Every step forward
is a surrender,
a release of the past
that clears the path for your future.

The Spark Within

There is a fire inside you
that burns brighter than any flame.
It is the spark of creation,
the essence of your being.
You may not always see it,
but it is there—
waiting to ignite,
to push you beyond the boundaries
you've set for yourself.
Embrace that fire,
for it is your true nature
shining through the darkness.

The Silence Speaks

In the stillness,
there are no distractions—
only truth.
We are so often lost in the noise of life
that we forget to listen
to the wisdom that comes from silence.
The world does not need more voices.
It needs more listeners.
It is in the quiet
that we hear our souls
and the whisper of the universe.

The Power of Choice

Every moment, you choose.
You choose your thoughts,
your words,
your actions.
You choose the direction of your life,
whether you realize it or not.
The power of choice is your birthright,
and within it lies the freedom
to create the life you desire.
So choose with intention,
with wisdom,
and with love.

The Road Less Traveled

The path you walk may not be easy,
but it is yours.
It is the road less traveled,
the one that challenges you
to grow,
to become,
to evolve.
Though others may take the easier way,
know that the journey you are on
holds a deeper meaning,
a purpose you have yet to fully understand.
Trust in the journey,
for it is leading you exactly where you need to go.

BEYOND THE VEIL

Through the Storm

When the storm rages,
do not seek shelter in fear.
For it is in the storm
that you are reborn.
The chaos is not your enemy,
but your teacher.
It shows you what you are made of,
what you are capable of enduring.
When the storm passes,
you will find yourself stronger,
wiser,
and more whole than you were before.

Trust the Flow

Life does not need to be controlled,
but rather,
trusted.
The river does not fight against the current,
it flows with it.
And in doing so,
it finds its way to the ocean.
So trust the flow of life,
even when it feels uncertain.
The path ahead may not always be clear,
but it will always lead you
where you are meant to go.

The Echo of Truth

Truth is not something you seek outside of yourself.
It is not a destination,
but a journey within.
When you speak your truth,
it resonates beyond words—
it echoes in the hearts of those who listen,
reminding them of their own truths.
It is not loud or brash,
but quiet and undeniable,
like the sound of the ocean
against the shore.
Always present,
always steady.

The Art of Becoming

You are always becoming.
In every moment,
in every breath,
you are changing,
growing,
evolving.

You are not static,
not fixed,
but a masterpiece in progress.

The artist does not rush the work—
it takes time,
patience,
and love.

And neither should you.

No matter your age,
no matter how much you've seen,
how much you think you know—
you are still unfolding.

There is no finish line,
no point at which you are complete.
Life will keep shaping you,
softening edges,
etching wisdom into your bones.

BEYOND THE VEIL

So do not say, I am done.
Do not limit yourself to what has been.
There is still more to learn,
more to see,
more to become.

Be patient with yourself,
for you are a living, breathing work of art,
forever in motion.

A Moment of Grace

Grace is not something you earn.
It is a gift,
given freely by the universe,
in moments of quiet surrender.
It is the feeling of being carried,
when you have no strength left.
It is the gentle reminder
that you are never alone,
even in your darkest hour.
Allow yourself to receive grace,
for it is the hand that lifts you up
when you least expect it.

The Blank Page

There are stories
within you,
waiting to be written.
They do not need
to be perfect,
only true.
Each word
is a piece of your soul,
each sentence
a step toward who you are meant to be.
Do not fear the blank page,
for it is an invitation,
a promise that your story
is yet to be told.

The Gift of Now

In the present,
we are whole.
In the present,
we are free.
The past is behind us,
the future yet to come,
but this moment,
this breath,
is all we need.
Take it in,
with all its beauty,
with all its grace,
for the present
is the gift we so often overlook.

The Sacred Pause

Before you act,
before you speak,
take a moment
to breathe.
In that sacred pause,
there is clarity.
In that stillness,
there is wisdom.
Do not rush through life—
let it unfold at its own pace,
for it is in the quiet moments
that we hear the whispers
of our deepest truths.

Walking Your Path

The road ahead may be unclear,
and the way may seem long,
but with each step,
you are guided.
The path was never meant
to be easy.
It was meant to challenge you,
to shape you,
to help you grow.
Trust your steps,
trust your heart,
and walk with the knowing
that you are never alone.

The Beauty of Imperfection

Perfection is a lie.
What is perfect,
anyway?
It is the cracks in the stone,
the rough edges of the world,
that hold the true beauty.
There is grace
in imperfection,
in the messy,
in the raw.
Do not seek perfection—
seek authenticity.
Seek the truth
in the way you are,
right here, right now.

The Language of the Soul

The soul does not speak in words,
but in feelings.
It does not need logic,
it needs understanding.
When you listen to your heart,
you hear the language of your soul.
It is not always clear,
not always easy to understand,
but it is always true.
Trust that language,
for it will lead you to the answers
you seek.

The Greatest Shift

True change is not loud.
It does not demand attention
or make a spectacle of itself.
It is quiet,
it is subtle,
it begins within.
The revolution of the soul
is not fought with force,
but with awareness,
with love,
with deep understanding.
It is the softest whisper
that creates the greatest shift.

The Call of the Wild

There is a wildness within you,
a force that cannot be tamed.
It is the spark of life,
the essence of freedom,
the call of the wild.
Do not silence it,
do not cage it,
for it is your birthright.
Let it run free,
let it guide you
to places unknown,
to experiences unimagined.
For in your wildness,
you will find your truest self.

The Weight of Words

Words are heavy.
They carry the weight of our thoughts,
our emotions,
our intentions.
A single word can heal,
or it can hurt.
A single sentence can uplift,
or it can break.
Choose your words wisely,
for they are the vessels
that carry your soul's essence
out into the world.

The Quiet Warrior

Strength is not always loud,
it is often found in silence.
The quiet warrior
does not seek battle,
but faces it with calm,
with grace,
with unwavering resolve.
It is in stillness
that we find our true power,
our true courage.
For the quiet warrior knows
that the greatest strength
is the ability to remain peaceful
amidst the storm.

The Silence Between Words

There's a silence
that exists in the space between words—
A quiet hum,
a hum that whispers truth
without needing to speak.
We fill it with noise,
but that silence,
it carries more than we'll ever know.

Beyond What We See

The world you see is only a shadow
of the truth that lies beneath.
The clouds that cover the sun
are nothing but illusions
created by the mind's eye.
When you dare to see beyond,
you'll find a universe of light
waiting to be embraced.

The Quiet Corners of Your Soul

The journey is not out there,
it never was.
It's within,
in the quiet corners of your soul,
where you'll find the answers
you were always searching for.
Not in the external,
but in the silence that calls you home.

Surrender to the Unknown

You walk with fear,
hands gripping the edge
of what you know,
terrified to let go.
But only when you release,
when you surrender to the unknown,
do you find the true power
of your being.

The Stillness in Chaos

Amidst the storm,
there is always stillness.
When the world is spinning out of control,
there is a place inside you
where peace always resides.
Find it,
anchor yourself there,
and let the chaos unfold around you
without disturbing the quiet strength within.

Seeds of Wisdom

Like seeds planted in the soil,
wisdom grows slowly,
gently taking root in the heart.
At times, it seems barren,
yet beneath the surface,
it's working its magic,
ready to bloom in its own time.

The Infinite Dance

You are both the dancer
and the dance.
The rhythm of your life is never wrong,
it simply flows with the Universe,
in patterns that echo the heartbeat of creation.
Don't try to control it.
Surrender to it,
and let it guide you in its infinite dance.

The Mirror of the Soul

Look into the mirror,
not of glass,
but of your soul.
You will see reflected there
everything you've ever been,
and everything you could become.
In its depth,
you are both the question
and the answer.

Unwritten

There are pages of your life
yet to be written.
The ink is still fresh,
the story unfolding in real time.
Let go of the fear
of not knowing the ending.
Trust that every chapter
is a step toward your truth.

Both the Beginning and the End

Time is not a line;
it is a circle.
The past echoes in the present,
and the future whispers from the shadows.
You are both the beginning and the end,
infinite, cyclical,
always returning to the same place
but never quite the same.

The Art of Presence

Right here,
right now,
you are exactly where you need to be.
Don't look back,
don't rush ahead.
The power is in the present moment,
in the breath,
in the pause between thoughts.
This is where life happens—
not in the past,
not in the future,
but right now.

Nurturing Growth

Change is like a seed,
it doesn't ask permission to grow.
It doesn't care whether the soil is ready,
whether the weather is favorable,
whether you have the strength to nurture it.
It simply grows,
unfolding as it was meant to,
in the time it was meant to.

There is no stopping it,
no avoiding it.
The more you try to control it,
the more it slips through your fingers,
yet, if you let go,
if you trust the process,
you will witness the beauty of transformation.

At first,
change is subtle,
a whisper beneath the surface.
Then, it grows louder,
stronger,
until it becomes undeniable.
You can either resist it,
in fear of the unknown,
or you can surrender to it,
knowing that it is leading you to where you are meant to be.

In the midst of change,

BEYOND THE VEIL

it's easy to forget that you are not broken.
You are simply being remade,
reimagined,
reborn.
The seed has always held within it the potential for greatness,
but it can only reach that potential through growth,
through transformation,
through change.

Embrace it,
for it is the universe unfolding itself within you,
and it is only through change that we become who we were always meant to
be.

Silence Speaks

There are words unspoken
in the silence between us.
Not every conversation needs to be loud
to be understood.
Sometimes, it is in the stillness
that the deepest truths are shared.

Listen to the quiet,
and hear what cannot be said
with mere words.

The Alchemy of Surrender

There is a magic in letting go,
a power in surrender.
You may think you are giving up control,
but in truth, you are returning to it—
you are returning to yourself.

The universe is vast,
and it has far more wisdom
than your ego could ever comprehend.
Trust it.
Trust that what is meant for you
will find its way.
And in surrender,
you will find your true strength.

The Mirror of Truth

There is a mirror,
but not the one you see in the reflection.
It is not the surface of your face,
not the lines and creases of your body,
but something far deeper.
The mirror of truth is not made of glass,
it is woven from the threads of your soul.

When you look into it,
you do not see yourself as you wish to be,
or as you have been told you are,
but as you truly are,
unfiltered,
raw,
and real.

In this mirror,
there is no hiding from yourself.
No pretension,
no illusion.
You will see every part of you,
the light and the dark,
the beautiful and the broken.
And in this truth,
there is freedom.

You will understand that nothing in you is wrong,
nothing in you is misplaced.
You are the perfect reflection of the universe,

BEYOND THE VEIL

as you are,
right now.

And once you see this,
once you truly understand it,
you will stop running from yourself.
You will stop seeking validation outside of your own heart,
and you will know that the love,
the truth,
the light,
was always within you,
waiting for you to look into that mirror
and remember.

A Soul's Journey

Your soul is not bound by time.
It exists beyond the linear path that you walk on earth,
it moves through dimensions,
through lifetimes,
through moments of pure consciousness.

It is not confined to the body,
though the body is its vessel.
The body is not the beginning,
nor the end,
it is simply the experience.
And your soul,
it is eternal.

The journey of the soul is not a path,
it is a spiral.
It twists and turns,
coming back again and again,
but never in the same way.
With each turn,
it gains wisdom,
it sheds old skins,
and it learns new lessons.

The journey is not about getting somewhere,
it is about becoming who you are meant to be.
It is the discovery of your essence,
the remembering of your divinity,
and the unfolding of your true potential.

BEYOND THE VEIL

As you walk this journey,
know that every step you take is part of a greater story,
a story that is infinite,
endless,
and filled with love.

Your soul knows the way,
it always has.
Trust it.
Listen to it.
And remember that you are not alone—
the entire universe walks with you,
guiding you,
protecting you,
loving you.

Beneath the Surface

We are all the same,
beneath the surface.
We are not defined by the roles we play,
or the masks we wear.
We are not the sum of our mistakes,
nor are we the stories others have told us.

Beneath the surface,
we are the same energy,
the same light,
the same divine source,
all connected by the threads of the universe.
It is only the surface that separates us,
the ego,
the illusion of individuality.

But if you look closely,
beneath the skin,
beneath the words,
beneath the chaos of the world,
you will see the truth:
we are all one.

And in that truth,
there is no judgment,
no separation,
no fear.
Only love,
only unity,

BEYOND THE VEIL

only peace.

We are all the same,
beneath the surface.
And when we remember that,
we will heal the world.

The Dance of Duality

Light and dark,
joy and pain,
love and fear—
they are two sides of the same coin.
Without one,
the other cannot exist.

You cannot know peace
without knowing chaos.
You cannot experience love
without experiencing loss.
And so, we dance
between these forces,
learning, growing, evolving.

Do not fight the duality of life.
Embrace it.
For it is through contrast
that you become whole.

All Things Flow

Everything moves in cycles,
everything flows.
The moon waxes and wanes,
the tide rises and falls,
and so do you.

There is no need to resist the ebb and flow,
for even in moments of stillness,
there is movement beneath the surface.
In the quiet, the seeds are being planted.
In the darkness, the roots are growing.

Know that you are part of this great flow,
and nothing is ever truly stagnant.
Trust the rhythm,
and surrender to the dance of life.

An Offering of Light

There is light in you
that no darkness can touch.
It burns quietly,
steadily,
from the deepest corners of your soul.
Even when you cannot see it,
it is there.
It is always there.

You may search for it outside of yourself,
but it is not hidden in the world.
It is not found in the places you visit,
nor in the people you encounter.
It is found in the stillness within,
in the space between your thoughts,
in the moments you let go of everything.

And when you discover it,
you will realize that the light you sought
was never separate from you.
It has been you all along.

Reborn

From the ashes,
you will rise.
Not as the person you once were,
but as the person you always were meant to be.
The fire does not destroy you,
it refines you.

What was once heavy
will become light.
What was once broken
will become whole.
And you will emerge from the flames,
stronger than you ever imagined.

Unshaken

I do not take your beliefs as my own,
do not wear your opinions like a cloak,
do not swallow your fears as if they were mine to carry.

Your reality is not my home.
The walls you build to define the world—
I do not live within them.

You see through the lens of your own becoming,
through wounds unhealed, through lessons learned,
but they are yours, not mine.

I will not shrink to fit your vision,
will not bow beneath the weight
of a truth that is not my own.

I stand unshaken, rooted in knowing—
not all voices deserve an echo,
not all maps lead to my destination.

I honor your path,
but I walk my own.

In the Quiet

In the quiet,
I find myself again.
The noise of the world fades away,
and I remember who I am,
what I came here to do.
The chatter of the mind
gives way to the voice of the soul.
And in that stillness,
I am whole.

The Heart Knows

The heart does not ask for permission.
It beats with an urgency
that cannot be ignored.
It knows the truth before the mind does,
it senses what is right,
what is aligned,
even when logic falters.

Follow your heart.
It is never wrong,
even when the world says otherwise.
The heart knows
what the ego cannot yet understand.

To Be Seen

To be seen,
truly seen,
is to be recognized in your fullest essence—
not for the roles you play,
or the masks you wear,
but for the truth that lives within you.

And when you allow yourself to be seen,
without fear,
without shame,
you give others permission to do the same.
It is in the act of vulnerability
that true connection is born.

The Silent Teacher

Silence speaks louder than words.
In the absence of sound,
you hear the whispers of your soul.
The stillness teaches
what words never could—
the power of presence,
the wisdom of being.

In silence,
you discover yourself
and the truth that lies within.

Embrace the Shadows

Do not fear the darkness,
for it is only in shadows
that light is born.
Without contrast,
we would never know depth,
we would never see the beauty
in the way light dances.

Embrace your shadows,
for they reveal your light.
Without them,
you would be incomplete.

Time Does Not Wait

Time does not wait for you
nor does it follow your commands.
It moves in its own rhythm,
sometimes slow,
sometimes swift,
but always forward.

Do not let time be your enemy.
Instead, let it remind you
that every moment is precious,
every breath is a gift.
Live fully,
for the weight of time is not
in its passing,
but in how you use it.

The River Within

There is a river within you,
flowing steady and deep,
carrying the wisdom of ages.
You may try to resist its current,
but it will always find its way.
It is in you,
the quiet voice of your soul,
leading you through life's twists and turns.

Trust the river.
It knows the path.
And though it may appear still,
it is never stagnant.

The Breath of Creation

Each breath you take
is an act of creation.
You breathe in the universe,
and with each exhale,
you shape it into something new.
Do not underestimate the power of breath,
for with it, you are both the creator
and the creation.

In every inhale,
you invite possibility.
In every exhale,
you release what no longer serves you.

Oneness

You are not separate from the world,
nor from the stars,
the trees,
the ocean,
or the sky.
You are part of the whole,
a single note in the song of existence.

Feel the connection.
In every person you meet,
in every animal you encounter,
in the rustling of leaves—
it is all you.

And when you remember this,
the world becomes a reflection of your soul,
and all that is, is sacred.

The Strength in Surrender

Surrender is not weakness,
it is strength.
To release control
is to trust the universe
to lead you in the right direction.
When you let go,
you are not giving up,
but allowing something greater than yourself
to carry you forward.

Let go of the need to force,
and you will find ease.
In surrender,
you will discover true power.

The Never Ending Journey

There is no destination,
no final point of arrival.
The journey is infinite,
always unfolding,
always evolving.

Every step you take,
every choice you make,
shapes the path,
but the journey itself—
it is not about the end.
It is about the becoming.
It is about growth.
It is about the lessons you learn
along the way.

So walk with an open heart,
and trust the journey.
For it is the most sacred part.

In the Waiting

In the waiting,
we grow.
It is not in the rushing
or the pushing forward,
but in the stillness
that we prepare ourselves
for what is to come.

The waiting is sacred.
It is where the seeds are planted.
And when the time is right,
they will bloom.

The Light Beyond the Storm

The storm will pass,
it always does.
And beyond it,
there is light.
It may be hidden behind dark clouds now,
but it is there.
It always has been.

When the wind howls,
when the rain pours,
trust that the storm is temporary.
And on the other side,
the sun will shine again.

You are not the storm.
You are the light that follows it.

The Language of the Heart

The heart does not speak in words,
but in rhythms,
in subtle movements,
in the feeling of a moment.

It is not bound by language,
for the heart understands something deeper,
something beyond the reach of the mind.
Listen closely,
and you will hear its song.

A Quiet Protest

Change does not always come
with loud proclamations,
with storms of protest.
Sometimes, it arrives
quietly,
like the soft unfolding of a new flower.

Change begins within.
It stirs the soul,
nudging you to transform,
and in time,
it ripples outward
into the world.

Through the Eyes of Love

Look at the world
through the eyes of love,
and you will see beauty
in the most unexpected places.
Even in the cracks,
the brokenness,
there is light.

It is love that gives meaning
to everything,
that transforms the mundane
into the miraculous.
Let love be your lens.
It will change the way you see.

The Sacred Dance of Life

Life is a dance.
Sometimes it's slow,
sometimes it's fast,
but always, it moves.
In every step,
there is a lesson,
a rhythm,
a flow.

Do not try to control the dance.
Let it carry you.
Surrender to the movement
and trust that the rhythm
will guide you where you need to go.

The Courage to Be Still

It takes courage to be still.
To sit with your thoughts,
with your emotions,
with the silence.
The world tells you to always be doing,
to always be moving,
but stillness is where clarity lives.

In stillness,
the answers come.
In stillness,
you find your truth.

The Fire of Transformation

The fire burns,
it cleanses,
it purifies.
What was once ash
becomes new life.

Do not fear the fire.
It is not destruction,
but a powerful force
that transforms everything it touches.
Let it burn away what no longer serves you,
and emerge from it
renewed.

Your True Self

When you look into the mirror,
what do you see?
Not the face,
not the body,
but the soul behind it.

The mirror reflects who you are,
who you have been,
and who you are becoming.
It shows you the truth
that is sometimes hidden
beneath the surface.

Look deeper,
and you will find
your true self staring back at you.

In Between Breaths

In the pause,
there is power.
In the stillness between breaths,
in the quiet moments before action,
the universe speaks.

Do not rush past the pause.
It is the space where creation begins,
where your soul aligns with the Divine.
In the pause,
you remember who you are.

The Garden of the Soul

Plant seeds of kindness,
water them with patience,
and let the garden of your soul grow.
In time,
you will see flowers bloom—
compassion, love,
understanding, and peace.

Tend to your garden every day,
and it will flourish.
The soul's garden is endless,
and it is always worth the effort.

The Symphony of Life

Life is a symphony,
with each moment a note,
each experience a chord.
You are the conductor,
guiding the orchestra of your existence.

Do not worry if the music falters,
if the tempo shifts.
Every moment,
whether joyous or painful,
is part of the song.
And in the end,
it will all come together
in perfect harmony.

The Silent Messenger

There are messages in silence,
carried not by words,
but by the stillness between breaths.
The universe speaks in quiet whispers,
only heard by those willing to listen.

In the silence, you find your truth.
In the pause, you discover your path.
Listen.
The answers are there, waiting.

The Dawn of Understanding

When the first light of understanding breaks,
it casts away the shadows of confusion.
What was once unclear now shines,
and you see the path ahead clearly.

But understanding is not a destination.
It is a continuous dawn,
slowly lighting the way.
And each step you take
will bring you closer to the truth.

A Breath of Peace

Take a breath.
Inhale deeply,
let the air fill your body.
Feel the peace that comes with each inhale,
each exhale.

In that breath,
you are one with everything.
In that moment,
there is no past,
no future.
Only now.

The Unseen Light

There is light within you,
though you may not always see it.
It is there,
hidden beneath layers of doubt,
fear,
and uncertainty.

But it is always shining,
even in the darkest of times.
Trust that the light is within,
and one day,
it will burn brighter than the sun.

The Path of Least Resistance

Sometimes, the hardest path
is the one that requires the least effort.
It is the path of surrender,
of letting go,
of trusting the flow.

Do not force your way through life.
Instead, allow yourself to be carried,
guided by the current of love,
of intuition,
of divine wisdom.

Embrace the Quiet

In the stillness of being,
you discover your essence.
Not in doing,
not in achieving,
but in simply being.

This is where you find peace,
where you find clarity,
where you find your true self.
Embrace the quiet.
It holds all that you need.

The Journey Inward

The journey outward is nothing compared to the journey inward.
What you seek in the world is already within you.
The answers, the wisdom, the peace,
they are all waiting for you to find.

Do not look outside yourself.
Look within.
And when you discover your own truth,
you will find the world you've been seeking all along.

The Strength of Softness

Strength is not always loud.
It is not always forceful.
Sometimes, it is soft,
gentle,
unseen.

Like a river carving its path through stone,
the strength of softness endures.
It is in the quiet moments,
the steady persistence,
the willingness to bend
without breaking.

The Courage to Evolve

Evolution is not easy.
It requires shedding old skins,
discarding comfort for growth.
But within every shift,
there is strength.

The courage to evolve
is not about fearlessness,
but the willingness to move forward
even with the uncertainty.
Trust the process.
You are becoming.

BEYOND THE VEIL

The Voice of the Soul

The soul does not speak in words.
It speaks in whispers,
in gut feelings,
in nudges that guide you to the truth.

Listen closely.
It knows the way.
And when you begin to trust its voice,
you will realize that every step
is part of a larger, divine design.

The Reflection of Others

Every person you meet
is a reflection of you.
Their words, their actions,
their energy,
mirror your own.

If you want to change the world,
start by changing yourself.
When you heal,
the world heals with you.
What you see in others
is what you are learning to see in yourself.

The Silence Between the Notes

Music is not only in the sound.
It is in the silence between the notes,
in the pauses where everything holds its breath,
waiting to be heard.

Life, too, is in the spaces.
In the moments of stillness,
in the gaps between thoughts,
in the breath you take before action.
There is meaning in the silence.

The Freedom of Release

Freedom is found not in possession,
but in letting go.
When you release the need to control,
the world opens up.

Trust that the universe will provide,
that Source will guide,
and that you are always exactly where you need to be.
Let go of what weighs you down,
and feel the lightness of your soul.

The Power of Gratitude

Gratitude shifts everything.
It turns what you have into enough,
what you lack into possibility.
It opens your eyes to the abundance
that surrounds you.

Gratitude is the key
to unlocking your joy,
to transforming your perspective,
to seeing the miracles that are always present.

The Light in the Darkness

Darkness is not something to fear.
It is where the light is born.
Without the night,
we would never know the brilliance of the stars.

In your own life,
you may face moments of shadow,
but know that within that darkness,
there is light waiting to emerge.
You are the light.

The Depth of Presence

Stillness is not emptiness.
It is a depth of presence,
a space where the soul can grow,
where the heart can heal,
where wisdom is birthed.

Do not be afraid of silence.
It is in that quiet,
that you will hear the loudest truths.
Stillness is where life begins.

The Echo of Knowing

You do not learn truth;
you remember it.
It stirs in your bones,
whispers in your pulse,
waits in the silence
between thoughts.

You have carried wisdom
long before you had words.
What you seek
is not outside you—
it has always been
a voice inside
longing to be heard.

The Shape of the Wind

You cannot see the wind,
but you know it is there.
You cannot hold it,
but you feel its touch.
It bends the trees,
moves the tides,
whispers through the hollow places.

So it is with love,
so it is with truth.
Not something to grasp,
but something to let move through you.

A World That Waits for Light

The world is not broken,
only waiting.
Waiting for hands
that do not turn to fists,
for voices
that do not sharpen into blades,
for eyes
that do not look away.

The world is waiting
for the ones who remember—
not how to conquer,
but how to heal.

Unfinished

You will never be complete.
Not in the way they told you.
Not like a puzzle
with pieces that finally fit.
You are not meant to be finished.

You are meant to stretch,
to unravel and reform,
to be endless in your becoming.
Do not seek the final version of yourself.
There isn't one.

An Offering to the Unknown

Do not fear what you cannot see.
The unknown is not emptiness;
it is possibility.
It is every road
not yet walked,
every door
not yet opened,
every version of you
that you have yet to meet.

Step forward—
not into darkness,
but into discovery.

BEYOND THE VEIL

The Sun in My Blood

They told me to hide from the sun,
but my body knows better.
The warmth on my skin
is an old remembering,
an ancient promise.

Like the trees,
like the flowers,
like every living thing that reaches—
I, too, was made for the light.

The Ones Who Do Not Fear the Mirror

The bravest ones
are not those who fight,
but those who turn inward
and face what they find.

It is easy to run,
to fill the silence with noise,
to drown the truth in distraction.

But the ones who look,
the ones who listen,
the ones who sit with themselves
and do not flinch—
they are the ones who wake up.

Rest is a Revolution

You were not born to be a machine.
You do not owe the world your exhaustion.

Rest is not laziness,
not a thing to earn.
It is your right,
your resistance,
your quiet defiance against a world
that tells you your worth
is only in what you produce.

Close your eyes.
Take up space in stillness.
You are enough,
even when you are not moving.

Begin Again

They gave you a name
before you could speak.
They gave you a path
before you could walk.

They built your walls
before you knew
you were meant to fly.

But the story they wrote for you
is not the one you have to live.
Rewrite. Unmake. Begin again.

Nothing Is Wasted

Not a tear,
not a heartbreak,
not a single moment
of breaking apart.

Every wound
has fed the soil of you.
Every sorrow
has stretched you open.

You are not ruined.
You are ripening.

BEYOND THE VEIL

To Those Who Have Been Called 'Too Much'

You are not too much.
The world has simply been
too small.

Your fire was never meant
to be contained.

Burn anyway.

Wintering

There is a season for stillness,
a time to turn inward
and gather yourself
like roots burrowed beneath the frost.

Let yourself slow.
Let yourself soften.

Spring will come.
It always does.

The Language of Energy

Before words,
before logic,
before the mind
could form its explanations—
there was knowing.

You do not need
to understand something
to feel its truth.

Trust what moves through you.

Dismantling the Illusion

They taught you to fear your power.
Taught you to kneel before systems
built to keep you asleep.

But the moment you see the strings,
the puppet show loses its hold.

Step beyond the illusion.
You were never meant to be controlled.

The Soul Remembers

Even if you forget,
even if the world
pulls you away from yourself,
there is something inside you
that never loses its way.

The soul does not need a map.
It simply knows.

Love Is Not a Cage

Love does not bind.
It does not hold you captive
or demand that you shrink
to fit inside its arms.

Love is the sky,
not the chain.
If it asks you to be small,
it is not love.

BEYOND THE VEIL

You Were Never Lost

You've spent lifetimes searching
for something you thought you lost.

A home. A purpose. A meaning.

But you were never lost—
just distracted by the noise.

Silence it.
Feel what has always been there.

The Fear of the Unknown

You stand at the edge,
paralyzed by what you cannot see.

But the unknown
is not darkness—
it is potential.

Everything beautiful
was once unknown.

Step forward.

The Art of Allowing

Stop fighting the river.
Stop trying to force the tide.

There is nothing to fix,
nothing to control.

Breathe.
Allow.

See how life unfolds
when you let it.

The Greatest Rebellion

No banners. No war cries.
No fire in the streets.

The greatest rebellion
is simply to wake up.

To question.
To unlearn.
To choose love
in a world built on fear.

Let It Break

Not everything is meant
to be held together.

Some things must break
so you can see
what was never whole to begin with.

Let it break.
Let it teach you.

You Are Not Behind

The timeline they gave you
was never yours to follow.

There is no late.
No early.
Only your own unfolding,
happening exactly as it should.

Trust it.

When the Old World Falls

The collapse is not the end.
It is the clearing.

Let the old world fall.
Let it crumble at your feet.

What you build next
is yours to decide.

The Sky Was Never the Limit

They told you to reach for the sky,
but the sky was never meant
to contain you.

You are meant to go beyond,
to expand,
to become more
than even you can imagine.

The sky was only the beginning.

What If You Stopped Running?

What if you turned around
and faced the thing
you've been running from?

What if it wasn't a monster,
but a door?

Some Things Are Not Yours to Carry

The weight on your shoulders
was never meant to be yours.

Put it down.

You do not need to carry
what is breaking you.

More Than This Moment

Whatever is heavy right now,
whatever is pressing on your chest—
remember:

This is not forever.
This is not the end.

You are more than this moment.

You Were Not Made to Shrink

You dim your light
so others feel comfortable.
You fold yourself smaller
to fit inside their expectations.

But you were not made to shrink.
You were made to take up space.

Let the Fire Burn

Not all destruction is loss.
Some things must burn
so that new life can grow.

Let the fire take what is already gone.
Stand in the ashes.
Watch yourself rise.

BEYOND THE VEIL

What If It Works Out?

Your mind whispers
all the ways it could go wrong.

But what if—
just this once—
it goes right?

Echoes of Another Life

Sometimes, in the quiet,
you hear something familiar—
a memory that doesn't belong to you,
a longing with no name.

Perhaps it is a life
you have lived before.

Or perhaps it is a life
still waiting for you.

Not Everything Needs an Explanation

Some things are not meant to be understood.
Some things are only meant to be felt.

Do not ruin the magic
by trying to name it.

BEYOND THE VEIL

When the Wind Calls Your Name

There will come a moment
when the world you built
no longer fits.

When the wind calls your name,
will you answer?

No One Else Can Walk This Path

They will try to tell you
which way to go,
what is right,
what is wrong.

But your path
is yours alone.

No one else
can walk it for you.

The Space Between

There is a pause,
a breath,
a space between the old and the new.

It is uncomfortable.
It is uncertain.
It is necessary.

Stay there.

BEYOND THE VEIL

Your Past Is Not Your Prison

You do not have to live there.
You do not have to be
who you were before.

You are allowed to grow.
You are allowed to change.

Your past is not your prison.

Some Doors Close for a Reason

Stop pounding on the door
that has already shut.

Some things end
because they were never meant to last.

Some doors close
to protect you.

You Will Survive This Too

You have survived every ending,
every heartbreak,
every moment you thought
you would not make it through.

And you will survive this too.

The Shape of Healing

Healing is not a straight road.
It twists, it loops back,
it circles the same wounds
you thought you had already mended.

One day, you wake up
and the weight is a little lighter.
The memories no longer sting.
You find yourself laughing again
without guilt.

It does not mean the past never happened.
It means you are no longer living there.

BEYOND THE VEIL

You Are Already Whole

They taught you to search for missing pieces—
to find another soul to complete you,
to seek something outside yourself
that was never truly lost.

But there is nothing missing.
There is no hole to fill.

You are already whole.
You always were.

BEYOND THE VEIL

The Unseen Thread

There is a thread, invisible to the eye,
that ties your soul to the places you have never been,
to the people you have yet to meet,
to the life that is already waiting for you.

Follow the pull.
It knows the way home.

The Silence Between the Notes

A song is not only the notes that are played—
it is also the silence between them.

Your life, too, needs space,
needs rest,
needs moments of stillness
so the music can breathe.

Do not be afraid of the silence.
It is part of the song.

Not Every Storm Is Meant to Break You

Some storms come to tear things down.
Some come to cleanse.
Some arrive only to shift you,
to push you where you were meant to be.

Not every storm is meant to break you.
Some storms come to set you free.

The Garden You Are Growing

Do not rush the blooming.
Some flowers take longer to unfurl,
some seeds remain buried for years
before they reach for the sun.

You are growing at your own pace.
Trust in the timing of your own becoming.

BEYOND THE VEIL

The Door That Was Never Locked

You stood before it for years,
waiting for someone to open it,
waiting for permission to walk through.

And then one day,
you reached out—
and the door was never locked.

BEYOND THE VEIL

You Were Always Meant to Find This

The words you needed,
the truth that would wake you,
the sign you were looking for—

It was always meant to find you.
And now, here you are.

The Places You Belong

Not every hand will hold you gently,
not every space will welcome your light.
But the places meant for you—
you will know them by the way
they feel like home.

The Echo of Who You Were

Sometimes, when the world quiets,
you hear the voice of who you used to be.
Not a ghost, not a mistake,
but a reminder
of how far you've come.

You do not have to erase them.
Let them walk beside you,
a witness to your becoming.

Roots Before Wings

Before the tree stretches toward the sky,
before the bird dares its first flight,
there is a deepening, a settling,
a trust in the unseen.

Grow your roots before you spread your wings.

BEYOND THE VEIL

The Truth Will Not Beg You

Truth does not chase,
does not plead to be believed.
It stands firm in the quiet,
waiting for you to be ready
to see it for what it is.

When the Universe Whispers

It does not shout.
It does not demand.
It speaks in soft nudges,
in gentle pulls,
in the feeling that will not leave you alone.

Listen.

A Quiet Unfolding

You will not wake up one day
and suddenly have it all figured out.
The becoming happens slowly—
a quiet unfolding,
a thousand tiny shifts
until one day you look back
and no longer recognize who you used to be.

BEYOND THE VEIL

Not Every Battle is Yours

There is wisdom in knowing
when to stand and fight—
and when to walk away.

Not every war belongs to you.

The Sky You Forgot to Look At

Today, you were busy.
Today, you carried too much.
Today, you hurried past the beauty
that stretched above you all along.

Lift your head.
The sky is still waiting.

The Language of Energy

Before words, before logic,
before the mind can explain—
the body knows.

You feel the answer
long before you hear it.
Learn to trust the language of energy.

Your Existence is Proof

You were not a mistake.
You are not random.
You are proof that the universe
wanted you here.

Breathe in that truth.

The Echo of Forgotten Dreams

Somewhere between sleep and waking,
where the veil is thin,
you remember the dreams you abandoned,
the whispers you silenced,
the roads you were too afraid to walk.

They call to you still,
like distant chimes in the wind,
asking if you will listen this time,
if you will let yourself want again,
if you will finally follow.

The Compass of Silence

They fear the silence
because in it, truth speaks.
Without noise to drown it,
without distractions to delay it,
the soul finally gets a voice.

But silence does not lie,
it does not distort,
it does not soften the edges
of what you have been avoiding.

It only points.
It only reveals.
It only waits for you to listen.

BEYOND THE VEIL

Chasing the Horizon

You were never meant to stay still,
to settle, to shrink,
to let the weight of comfort steal your hunger.

The horizon calls your name,
a voice in the wind,
a pulse beneath your skin.

And though you may never reach it,
you must go anyway.
Not to catch it—
but to remember you were born to run.

When the River Resists the Ocean

The river fights the ocean at first,
afraid to lose itself,
afraid to dissolve into something greater.

But the current is inevitable.

And when it surrenders,
it does not disappear—
it expands.

The Hands That Built You

Every touch you have known,
gentle or cruel,
has shaped you.

Every word whispered,
every hand held,
every door slammed shut—
they all left fingerprints
on the clay of your soul.

But the sculpture is yours to finish.
You choose what remains,
what is softened,
what is chiseled away.

You are not just what was done to you.
You are what you create from it.

You Are All

You are not just the seed,
but the soil,
the storm,
the sun that coaxes life from the dark.

You are not just the canvas,
but the brush,
the color,
the trembling hand
that dares to paint something new.

Becoming is both destruction and creation.
It is messy.
It is raw.
It is holy.

And it is yours.

The Bones of the Earth

Lie down in the grass.
Feel the pulse beneath you.

This earth,
this ancient body,
has known every secret,
heard every prayer,
felt every tear
that ever fell upon it.

And still, it endures.

And so will you.

Wildflowers and Wounds

The places you were broken
will bloom one day.

Not because pain is beautiful,
but because you are.

Because even the deepest wounds
cannot stop the light from getting in,
cannot stop you from growing toward it.

You were never meant to stay buried.

BEYOND THE VEIL

The Alchemy of Fear

Fear is not the enemy.

It is a spark.
A fire in your hands,
burning only when resisted,
guiding when embraced.

Let it move you,
but never control you.
Let it warn you,
but never chain you.

Fear, when mastered,
becomes courage.

The Language of Trees

The trees do not hurry,
yet they stretch beyond measure.
They do not resist the wind,
yet they stand through storms.

They do not chase the sun,
yet they are always reaching.

If you listen,
they will teach you—
how to root,
how to bend,
how to grow without fear.

Unwritten Chapters

You are not just the pages behind you.
You are the ink in your hands,
the next breath,
the next step,
the next unwritten word.

Let the past be the prologue.
Let today be the turning point.

You are still holding the pen.

Saltwater Baptism

Let the waves take it.
The weight of yesterday,
the regrets heavy in your chest.

Wade into the tide
until you remember—
the ocean does not cling,
and neither should you.

Let it all go.

The Shape of Healing

Healing is not a straight road.
It is a spiral, a tide,
a dance between breaking and mending.

Some days, you will feel whole.
Some days, you will feel undone.
Both are part of the process.

Keep going anyway.

BEYOND THE VEIL

Where the Wild Things Grow

Beyond the fences of fear,
outside the walls of expectation,
there is a field where the wild things grow.

No rules, no maps,
just instinct and sky.

That is where you belong.

Sunlight Through the Cracks

You thought you were broken.
Fractured beyond repair.

But when the light found you,
it did not turn away.
It poured through the cracks,
painting gold where you thought
only emptiness remained.

You were never broken.
Just open.

A Love Letter to the Present Moment

Here.
This breath.
This heartbeat.
This sky.

Not yesterday,
not tomorrow,
but this—
this is life unfolding in your hands.

Hold it gently.
Hold it with awe.

The Universe Remembers

You have forgotten who you are,
but the universe has not.

It whispers in the wind,
writes it in the stars,
weaves it into the rivers.

You are not lost—
only remembering.

The Things You Will Not Regret

You will not regret
pausing to watch the sunset.

You will not regret
saying the words you were afraid to say.

You will not regret
choosing love over fear,
truth over comfort,
presence over distraction.

You will not regret
living fully,
even when it was messy.

A Feather on the Wind

Let go of the need to know,
the need to control,
the need to force.

Be like the feather on the wind.

Drifting, trusting,
dancing with the unseen currents,
knowing it will land
exactly where it is meant to be.

The Echo of Silence

Sometimes the most powerful words
are not spoken.

Sometimes the truth is in the quiet,
in the space between breaths,
in the pause before action.

The echo of silence is louder
than the noise you think you need.

Alchemy of Gold

Change is not the enemy.
It is the process of transformation.

It is the fire that refines the gold,
the storm that carves the mountain,
the wind that reshapes the landscape.

Let it burn,
let it blow,
let it shift—
it is only alchemy.

A Shift in the Soil

Sometimes you must dig deeper
to find the roots of your soul.

The soil may feel cold,
but beneath it,
life is stirring.

The seed has always been within you—
now it's time to bloom.

Dancing in the Dark

It is not always in the light
that we find our rhythm.

Sometimes it's the dark
that teaches us how to move—
how to trust our inner pulse,
how to navigate without sight.

Dancing in the dark,
we discover the depth of our own soul.

The Fire Within

Do not wait for the world to light your path.
Become the fire you seek.

Ignite the spark within you
and watch as it spreads—
a blaze that cannot be ignored,
a warmth that others will seek.

The Space Between Thoughts

There is a space between every thought—
a quiet pause,
a breath,
a place where the mind does not chase,
where the heart just is.

In that space,
you will find clarity.
In that space,
you will find peace.

The Heart's True North

Follow the compass of your heart,
for it is always pointing you
toward your true north.

No map, no guide,
no earthly voice
can lead you as it can.

Trust the pull,
and you will never be lost.

BEYOND THE VEIL

A Garden in the Storm

Even in the storm,
there is a garden growing.

Though the wind howls and the rain falls,
the roots still dig deep,
the flowers still reach for the sun.

You are that garden—
unshaken,
unbroken,
always blooming.

Between the Moments

The moments that change us
are not always the big ones.
Sometimes it's the soft,
silent,
in-between moments
that shift the course of our lives.

Pay attention to them.
They are where magic hides.

The Courage to Begin Again

You do not need to have it all figured out.
You do not need to wait for the perfect moment.

Sometimes, the bravest thing you can do
is begin again.

Trust yourself.
Take that first step.
The journey will unfold.

The Hidden Path

Not all paths are visible.
Some must be felt,
walked with intuition
rather than sight.

Trust your feet to guide you,
for the hidden path
is always the truest one.

The Gift of Uncertainty

Uncertainty is a gift,
wrapped in the unknown.

It asks you to surrender,
to trust the unfolding,
to walk without knowing the steps.

There is beauty in the uncertainty.
It is the space where growth happens.

The Weight of the Stars

The stars do not carry the weight
of the universe—
they carry the light.

And so must you.
Lighten the load,
and let your radiance fill the sky.

Under the Surface

What you see is never the full picture.
Dig deeper,
look beyond the surface,
and you'll find the roots,
the truth,
the pulse of life.

The Breath Between Worlds

There is a breath between worlds—
a moment suspended
where everything and nothing exist.

Breathe into that space,
and know that you are both infinite and finite.

The Unspoken Truth

Not everything needs to be said.
Some truths are felt,
whispered between souls,
carried by energy,
understood in silence.

You know this truth.
It's always been with you.

A Canvas Unfinished

Your life is an unfinished canvas.
Every brushstroke
adds depth and color.

Do not fear the empty spaces—
they are where the next masterpiece is born.

The Wisdom of Silence

There is wisdom in silence—
not the absence of words,
but the presence of presence.

In silence, you can hear the world speak,
and in the quiet, you will find clarity.

Unraveling the Layers

Every day, we unravel a layer of ourselves.
The past, the present,
all unravel together,
each layer more revealing
than the last.

Do not fear what is exposed.
You are becoming your truest form.

The Universe in Your Hands

The universe is not far from you—
it is in your hands.

Every thought, every action,
creates ripples across infinity.
You are a creator,
a vessel of power,
and the universe listens.

BEYOND THE VEIL

The Shadow of Your Truth

Your truth is not always comfortable.
It casts shadows,
it stirs the dust,
it unsettles what was once still.

But in those shadows,
you will find your strength.
Do not fear them.

The Light You Carry

You do not need to find the light—
it is already within you.

Like the moon reflects the sun,
you reflect the Divine.
Carry your light with pride,
and let it illuminate your way.

The Dance of Opposites

Life is a dance of opposites—
light and dark,
love and fear,
creation and destruction.

Embrace both,
for without one, the other cannot exist.
In the dance, we find balance.

The Waiting Room

The waiting room is not a place of idleness.
It is a space of preparation,
of becoming,
of aligning with what is coming.

Do not rush the process.
The best things take time.

The Infinite Within

Within you is an infinite expanse—
a universe waiting to be explored.

Do not limit yourself to the smallness
that others have imposed.
You are vast,
and your potential is boundless.

The Thread of Destiny

Destiny is a thread,
woven through every moment,
connecting you to the past, the present,
and all that is yet to come.

Trust in the thread,
for it leads you where you are meant to go.

The Quiet Power of Reflection

In moments of reflection,
we find our true power.

It is in stillness that we connect with Source,
that we remember who we truly are,
and what we are capable of becoming.

The Pulse of Time

Time moves with an invisible pulse,
beat by beat,
rippling through the fabric of existence.

In each moment, there is a chance to listen,
to align your own rhythm with the pulse of the universe.

Do not rush,
for time is not something to chase.
It is something to feel,
to honor,
to dance with.

BEYOND THE VEIL

The Horizon of Possibilities

There is a horizon beyond the horizon—
a space where your dreams are waiting
to take form.

Do not limit your vision to what is close;
stretch your gaze further,
beyond the familiar,
beyond the fear,
and into the boundless potential
that calls you forward.

The Eternal Now

The past and the future are mere illusions.
What is real,
what is solid,
is the present moment,
the eternal now.

In the now, there is peace,
there is freedom,
there is everything you need.

Let go of the distractions,
the what-ifs and could-have-beens,
and anchor yourself in the only reality that exists.

The Alchemy of Change

Change is the greatest alchemy—
it transforms the base into gold,
the ordinary into extraordinary,
the unknown into wisdom.

Embrace change,
for it is through change that we grow,
that we become
who we are meant to be.

BEYOND THE VEIL

The Power of the Unseen

The most powerful forces are often unseen—
the wind, the earth, the energy that binds us all.

What you cannot see is often more real than what you can touch,
and it is in the invisible spaces
where the deepest connections are made.

Do not dismiss the unseen;
it is the foundation of all things.

The Strength of the Quiet

There is strength in the quiet.
It is in the stillness that we gather ourselves,
that we listen to the whispers of wisdom,
and that we learn to stand firm in our truth.

Sometimes the loudest voices are not the most powerful.
It is the quiet ones that hold the deepest strength,
rooted and unwavering.

Becoming the Storm

You are both the storm and the calm,
the thunder and the silence between.

It is in the tempest that you learn to surrender,
and in the stillness that you gather your strength.

Embrace the storm within you,
for it will shape you,
mold you,
and remind you of your power.

BEYOND THE VEIL

The Beauty of Impermanence

Nothing lasts forever,
and that is what makes everything beautiful.

It is in the fleeting nature of moments
that we find their true worth.

Do not cling to what will pass,
but savor it in its fullness,
and allow the next moment to come.

The Thread of Connection

Every person, every being,
is a thread in the grand tapestry of life.

We are all connected,
woven together by the invisible threads of love,
of compassion,
of shared experience.

Do not forget your thread—
it is part of something greater.

The Ocean of Wisdom

Wisdom is an ocean,
vast and deep,
endless and ever-moving.

Dive in,
lose yourself in its depths,
and you will emerge with treasures beyond measure.

But remember,
the ocean is not conquered,
it is embraced.

In Your Breath

Creation is not a singular act.
It is a continuous breath,
flowing in and out of existence.

You are a creator,
breathing life into every moment,
bringing forth beauty from the unseen.

In every breath, there is a new beginning.

The Courage to Wander

Wandering is not aimless—
it is the courage to explore the unknown,
to seek what is yet unseen.

Do not fear the wanderer within you.
Let them lead you to places that will change you,
shape you,
and remind you of your vast potential.

The Song of the Soul

Your soul sings a song,
soft and constant,
though you may not always hear it.

It is a melody of love,
of purpose,
of truth.

Listen closely,
and you will know your song,
and the world will hear it, too.

The Legacy of Love

At the end of this journey,
what remains is not the things we've done,
but the love we've shared.

The legacy of love is eternal,
it lives on in the hearts of those we touch,
in the ripples we leave behind.

Choose love,
and leave a legacy
that will never fade.

About the Author

Drew Mackby Sand is a Canadian writer and artist whose creative journey began in his teens with the publication of his first work. This early achievement sparked a lifelong passion for both artistic expression and academic exploration. With multiple art degrees and a multifaceted career in various creative disciplines, Drew has dedicated his life to his craft.

A self-described "black sheep," Drew's writing and poetry serve as his primary avenue for deep self-expression, reflecting his unique perspective and soulful introspection. His evocative, heartfelt poetry creates a powerful connection with readers, as he captures the raw emotions, experiences, and reflections that shape his world.

Through his imaginative spirit and authenticity, Drew invites readers to join him on a journey of discovery, offering a glimpse into the profound landscapes of his creativity and inner thoughts.

www.ingramcontent.com/pod-product-compliance
Lightning Source LLC
Chambersburg PA
CBHW070543010526
44118CB00012B/1204